Wilson Reading System®

Student Workbook Nine A

Wilson works.

THIRD EDITION

by Barbara A. Wilson

Wilson Language Training Corporation
www.wilsonlanguage.com

Wilson Reading System® Student Workbook Nine A

Item # SW9A

ISBN 978-1-56778-090-1

THIRD EDITION (revised 2004)

The Wilson Reading System is published by:

Wilson Language Training Corporation
47 Old Webster Road
Oxford, MA 01540
United States of America

(800) 899-8454

www.wilsonlanguage.com

Printed in the U.S.A.

July 2006

Select a vowel combination from the top of each box to form real words. Write the letters on the lines. Use a dictionary or electronic spell checker as needed. Read the words.

ai   ay
Sund____
f____nt
subw____

ai   ay
d____sy
rem____n
spr____

ai   ay
tr____l
runw____
p____nting

ai   ay
del____
gr____n
afr____d

ai   ay
p____ment
r____sin
rep____r

ai   ay
pl____pen
expl____n
Thursd____

Read the words below.

crayon	decade	station
daily	birthday	airplane
flavor	David	paper
space	rainfall	Thursday
explain	subway	dainty

Write the words in the correct columns below. If a word has two /ā/ spellings, write it in more than one column.

a	a-e	ai	ay
_____	_____	_____	_____
_____	_____	_____	_____
_____	_____	_____	_____
_____		_____	_____
		_____	

Fill in the correct spelling option for the /ā/ sound to complete each word.

a, a-e, ai, or ay?

spr___   t___ble   pl___n___

cel e br___t___   re m___n   ar c___d___

f___nt   hol i d___   re p___r

cr___v___   ex pl___n   trans por t___tion

d___time   re l___   st___tion

Write the words above in the correct columns below.

a	a-e	ai	ay
_____	_____	_____	_____
_____	_____	_____	_____
_____	_____	_____	_____
	_____	_____	_____

airport	complain	daisy	painful	entertaining
subway	birthday	relay	repair	explain

1 Mom gets upset when we _____ about her lunches.

2 Kelly Perkins will celebrate her fifth _____ on next Sunday.

3 Mike is _____ when he sings and dances for fun.

4 Ferdinand went to the _____ to get a plane to Cleveland.

5 Doris is helping her brother _____ his bike.

6 The kids like to play a _____ game at recess.

7 The doctor will prescribe a medication for that _____ _____ spot on *your* arm.

8 Can you _____ why birds fly to Florida in the winter?

9 Martin picked the _____ and gave it to Jenna.

10 Every major city has a _____ for public transportation.

Divide each word below into syllables. Mark the vowels. Use each word in a sentence and write it on the line.

EXAMPLE: <u>prō</u> <u>clāim</u>
    o   d

1 birthday   _____ _____

_____

2 runway   _____ _____

_____

3 explain   _____ _____

_____

4 relay   _____ _____

_____

5 dainty   _____ _____

_____

6 mermaid   _____ _____

_____

7 entertain   _____ _____ _____

_____

8 railway   _____ _____

_____

Choose a vowel combination from the top of each box to form real words. Use a dictionary or electronic spell checker as needed. Write the letters on the lines

ee   ey
troll____
ind____d
coff____

ee   ey
sixt____n
kidn____
disagr____

ee   ey
hock____
chim____
sl____ve

ee   ey
donk____
scr____ch
jers____

Write the words above on the lines below. Read the words.

ee	ey
_____	_____
_____	_____
_____	_____
_____	_____
_____	_____

Fill in the correct spelling option for the /ē/ sound to complete each word. Use a dictionary or electronic spell checker as needed.

e, e-e, y, ee, or ey?

dai l___   ch___k   val l___

jer s___   pr___tend   a gr___

sp___ch   r___main   troll___

d___cide   lad___   dai s___

cand___   dun ga r___   tur k___

Write the words above in the correct columns below.

---

e	**y**
_____	_____
_____	_____
_____	_____

ee	**ey**
_____	_____
_____	_____
_____	_____

Divide each word below into syllables. Mark the vowels. Use each word in a sentence and write it on the line.

EXAMPLE: *prō claim*
  o   d

1 referee

_____ _____ _____

_____

2 engineer

_____ _____ _____

_____

3 between

_____ _____

_____

4 thirteen

_____ _____

_____

5 teepee

_____ _____

_____

6 volunteer

_____ _____ _____

_____

7 parakeet

_____ _____ _____

_____

8 valley

_____ _____

_____

Read the words below. Underline or "scoop" the syllables. Mark the vowels. Circle the vowel combination.

EXAMPLE: dō maîn
    o   d

kidney	November	donkey
between	fifteen	indeed
subway	Hershey	needle
sixteen	needle	chimney
repair	relay	hockey
coffee	agree	toffee
chimpanzee	beehive	referee
decide	summer	railway
airplane	pewee	entertain
asleep	committee	exercise

Read the syllables on each side of the box. Draw a line to join the syllables to form real words.

tur	zers
kid	key
twee	ney

be	ley
val	teen
nine	tween

trol	deed
in	dom
free	ley

chim	hive
bee	ney
jer	sey

Write the words above on the lines below. Read the words.

Select a vowel combination from the top of each box to form real words. Write the letters on the lines.

oa   oe
cockr____ch
charc____l
t____ster

oa   oe
coc____
thr____t
t____s

oa   oe
tipt____
b____rd
d____

oa   oe
h____
t____st
appr____ch

oa   oe
c____sting
c____ch
t____

oa   oe
c____l
fl____t
cardb____rd

Fill in the correct spelling option for the /ō/ sound to complete each word. Use a dictionary or electronic spell checker as needed.

What says /ō/?

1 _____ **2** _____ **3** _____ **4** _____

s___p	thr___t	r___dent	d___
r___d block	h___m___	dom i n___	pho t___ graph
t___	ph___n___	c___ch	pr___tect
f___m	mi cro sc___p___		tip t___

Write the words above in the correct columns below.

oe

_____

_____

_____

o-e

_____

_____

_____

oa

_____

_____

_____

_____

o

_____

_____

_____

Read the sentences below. Locate and correct the misspelled words by writing the proper spelling above the misspelled one. Use a dictionary or electronic spell checker as needed.

1 joan went fishing in the blue bote

2 did the coatch think it was a gole

3 i like to flote on the raft and soke my toes in the rivver

4 we must get some charcole to have a barbecu

5 will sue come visit on tuesda

Write the sentences correctly on the lines below. Proofread them carefully.

1 _____

_____

2 _____

_____

3 _____

_____

4 _____

_____

5 _____

_____

Read the words below. Underline or "scoop" the syllables and circle the **ue** in each word. Determine the sound of **ue**: /ū/ or /ü/.

EXAMPLE: <u>res</u> <u>cue</u>

true	due	argue	fondue
overdue	avenue	rescue	clue
Tuesday	barbecue	Sue	value
continue	glue	blue	

Write the words above in the correct columns below.

ue says /ū/   **ue** says /ü/

_____   _____

_____   _____

_____   _____

_____   _____

                                    _____

                                    _____

                                    _____

educate	argue	cute	stupid
refuse	reduce	true	tulip
humid	mule	rescue	tube
Tuesday	rule	pupil	student
continue	blue		

What says /ū/?

1 _____ **2** _____ **3** _____

_____ _____ _____

_____ _____ _____

_____ _____ _____

What says /ü/?

1 _____ **2** _____ **3** _____

_____ _____ _____

_____ _____ _____

_____ _____ _____

Choose a vowel combination from the top of each box to form real words. Write the letters on the lines. Use a dictionary or electronic spell checker as needed.

oi   oy
t____
sirl____n
destr____

oi   oy
enj____ment
l____al
p____nt

oi   oy
t____let
ch____ce
cordur____

oi   oy
p____son
br____ler
paperb____

Write the words above on the lines below. Read the words.

oi	**oy**
_____	_____
_____	_____
_____	_____
_____	_____
_____	_____

Choose a vowel combination from the top of each box to form real words. Write the letters on the lines. Use a dictionary or electronic spell checker as needed.

au **aw**
f____cet
d____n
cr____fish

au **aw**
h____nt
squ____k
s____ce

au **aw**
astron____t
r____hide
l____ndry

au **aw**
dr____
f____lt
____ful

Write the words above on the lines below. Read the words.

au	**aw**
_____	_____
_____	_____
_____	_____
_____	_____
_____	_____

Divide each word below into syllables. Mark the vowels. Use each word in a sentence and write it on the line.

EXAMPLE: craw fish
d   c

1 faucet _____ _____

_____

2 sawdust _____ _____

_____

3 author _____ _____

_____

4 astronaut _____ _____ _____

_____

5 August _____ _____

_____

6 laundry _____ _____

_____

7 saucer _____ _____

_____

8 strawberry _____ _____ _____

_____

Read the syllables in the boxes. Draw a line to connect syllables to form real words.

tom	joice
re	foil
tin	boy

sir	loin
laun	joy
en	dry

jig	stroy
de	cer
sau	saw

loy	on
pois	ter
oys	al

Write the words above on the lines below. Read the words.

_____   _____

_____   _____

_____   _____

_____   _____

_____   _____

Read the sentence. Select the correct word from the box to complete the sentence. Write the word on the line. Reread the completed sentence. Use each word in the box only once.

tinfoil	August	haunted	appointment	strawberry

1 Mom will make _____ shortcake for my birthday party.

2 It is hot in _____ so we will be able to swim in the lake.

3 We can cover the casserole with _____ to protect it from the dust in the air.

4 Joe has a dentist _____ at twelve o'clock.

5 I think this is a _____, old attic!

Rewrite the sentences correctly on the lines below. Proofread them carefully.

1 _____

2 _____

3 _____

4 _____

5 _____

Choose a vowel combination from the top of each box to form real words. Use a dictionary or electronic spell checker as needed. Write the letters on the lines.

ou   ow
s____nd
cr____n
p____der

ou   ow
tr____sers
fr____n
am____nt

ou   ow
p____nce
all____
cr____ch

ou   ow
cr____d
ch____der
disc____nt

Write the words above on the lines below. Read the words.

ou	ow
_____	_____
_____	_____
_____	_____
_____	_____
_____	_____

Divide the words and write the syllables on the lines. Mark the syllable types and vowels. Read the words. Write the sound of **ow** in the bars (/ō/ or /ou/). Use a dictionary or electronic spell checker as needed for the sound of **ow**.

EXAMPLE: <u>el</u> <u>b(ow)</u> <u>/ō/</u>
     c   d

follow = ___ ___ /__/   minnow = ___ ___ /__/

chowder = ___ ___ /__/   tower = ___ ___ /__/

shallow = ___ ___ /__/   vowel = ___ ___ /__/

elbow = ___ ___ /__/   arrow = ___ ___ /__/

pillow = ___ ___ /__/   powder = ___ ___ /__/

shower = ___ ___ /__/   rainbow = ___ ___ /__/

flower = ___ ___ /__/   drowsy = ___ ___ /__/

snowball = ___ ___ /__/   borrow = ___ ___ /__/

drowsy = ___ ___ /__/   below = ___ ___ /__/

window = ___ ___ /__/   power = ___ ___ /__/

Read the sentence. Select the correct word from the box to complete the sentence. Write the word on the line. Reread the completed sentence. Use each word in the box only once.

| rooster | smooth | poodle | cartoons | raccoons |

1 The _____ provide entertainment on Saturday mornings.

2 Dad sanded the table until it felt _____.

3 The _____ frequently get into the trash barrels in the park.

4 That pet _____ is quite a spoiled dog.

5 Gail thinks there are many hens and one _____ on that small farm.

Write the sentences above on the lines below. Underline or "scoop" the syllables in multisyllabic words. Mark the vowel digraph/diphthong syllables and circle the **oo** vowel combinations.

1 _____

2 _____

3 _____

4 _____

5 _____

Divide the words and write the syllables on the lines. Mark the syllables on the lines. Mark the syllable types and vowels. Read the words. Write the sound of **oo** in the bars (/ü/ or /u̇/).

EXAMPLE: **loop hōle**
　　　　　　d　　v-e

fishhook	= ___ ___ /__/	afternoon =	_ _ ___ /__/
bamboo	= ___ ___ /__/	shampoo =	___ ___ /__/
notebook	= ___ ___ /__/	booklet =	___ ___ /__/
woodshed	= ___ ___ /__/	raccoon =	___ ___ /__/
mushroom	= ___ ___ /__/	hookup =	___ ___ /__/
rooster	= ___ ___ /__/	driftwood =	___ ___ /__/
scooter	= ___ ___ /__/	cartoon =	___ ___ /__/
balloon	= ___ ___ /__/	childhood =	___ ___ /__/
football	= ___ ___ /__/	footing =	___ ___ /__/
poodle	= ___ ___ /__/	igloo =	___ ___ /__/

Read the words. Determine the sound of the underlined letters. List the words in the correct spaces according to the underlined sounds. Use a dictionary or electronic spell checker as needed.

m<u>oo</u>n   cr<u>ow</u>n   holl<u>ow</u>   thundercl<u>ou</u>d

gr<u>ou</u>nd   c<u>ou</u>gar   t<u>ow</u>er   c<u>ou</u>pon

disc<u>ou</u>nt   arr<u>ow</u>   ball<u>oo</u>n   cr<u>oo</u>k

s<u>ou</u>p   underst<u>oo</u>d   Hall<u>ow</u>een   m<u>oo</u>se

h<u>oo</u>ked   ch<u>ow</u>der

What says /**ou**/?

1 _____   2 _____   3 _____

_____   _____   _____

_____   _____   _____

What says /ō/?

1 _____   2 _____   3 _____   4 _____   5 _____

_____   _____   _____

What says /ü/?

1 _____   2 _____   3 _____   4 _____   5 _____

_____   _____   _____

_____   _____   _____

What says /u̇/?

1 _____

_____   _____

Divide each word below into syllables. Mark the vowels. Use each word in a sentence and write it on the line.

EXAMPLE eas y
d o

1 eagle _____ _____

_____

2 eastern _____ _____

_____

3 increase _____ _____

_____

4 peacock _____ _____

_____

5 beaver _____ _____

_____

6 defeat _____ _____

_____

7 reason _____ _____

_____

8 beneath _____ _____

_____

Divide the words and write the syllables on the lines. Mark the syllable types and vowels. Read the words. Write the sound of **ea** in the bars (/ĕ/ or /ē/). Use a dictionary or electronic spell checker to determine the **ea** sound as needed.

EXAMPLE: <u>un</u> <u>real</u> /ē/
     c   d

feather = ___ ___ /__/	increase = ___ ___ /__/
peanut = ___ ___ /__/	instead = ___ ___ /__/
heaven = ___ ___ /__/	teaspoon = ___ ___ /__/
steamer = ___ ___ /__/	weather = ___ ___ /__/
meadow = ___ ___ /__/	reason = ___ ___ /__/
leather = ___ ___ /__/	season = ___ ___ /__/
eagle = ___ ___ /__/	displease = ___ ___ /__/
breakfast = ___ ___ /__/	ahead = ___ ___ /__/
sweater = ___ ___ /__/	seacoast = ___ ___ /__/
defeat = ___ ___ /__/	easy = ___ ___ /__/

Choose a vowel combination from the top of each box to form real words. Use a dictionary or electronic spell checker as needed. Write the letters on the lines.

ee ea
l___sh
tr___t
j___p

ee ea
asl___p
t___cup
b___

ee ea
b___tle
b___gle
sevent___n

ee ea
h___t
sl___ve
p___ce

Write the words above on the correct lines below. Read the words.

ee

ea

_____

_____

_____

_____

_____

_____

_____

_____

_____

_____

Proofread each sentence. Correct the spelling of the underlined words. Rewrite each sentence correctly on the lines provided. Add capital letters and punctuation.

1   barney is ed's <u>beagl</u> <u>pupy</u>

_____

_____

2   the <u>docter</u> told gail to increase her <u>slepe</u>

_____

_____

3   did you <u>lik</u> the <u>penut</u> butter and <u>jely</u> sandwich

_____

_____

4   have you ever <u>visitid</u> the eastern <u>seeshore</u>

_____

_____

5   the <u>beever</u> was underneath a pile of cut <u>treas</u>

_____

_____

Circle all the **ea** letter combinations in the words below. Determine the sound of **ea** (/ĕ/ or /ē/). Write the sound above the circled letters.

EXAMPLE: br**ea**d /ĕ/

health	seat	already	dream
treat	mean	beagle	leather
meadow	bread	head	ahead
speak	teacher	stream	instead
eat	thread		

Write the words above in the correct columns below.

ea = /ē/

ea = /ĕ/

Divide the words and write the syllables on the lines. Mark the syllable types and vowels. Read the words. Write the sound of **ew** in the bars (/ü/ or /u̇/). Use a dictionary or an electronic spell checker as needed.

pewter = ___ ___ /__/   Lewis = ___ ___ /__/

unscrew = ___ ___ /__/   newscast = ___ ___ /__/

renew = ___ ___ /__/   dewdrop = ___ ___ /__/

outgrew = ___ ___ /__/   newborn = ___ ___ /__/

sewer = ___ ___ /__/   Brewster = ___ ___ /__/

nephew = ___ ___ /__/   jewel = ___ ___ /__/

cashew = ___ ___ /__/   mildew = ___ ___ /__/

Write the words above on the lines below.

_____   _____

_____   _____

_____   _____

_____   _____

_____   _____

Proofread each sentence. Correct the spelling of the underlined words. Rewrite each sentence correctly on the lines provided. Add capital letters and punctuation.

1   the children <u>outgru</u> the <u>sumer</u> clothes

_____

_____

2   is there mildew on the <u>batroom</u> <u>sinc</u>

_____

_____

3   andrew never reads the <u>newspapper</u> but lewis always <u>reeds</u> it

_____

_____

4   roy blew the <u>canddles</u> out and <u>maid</u> a wish

_____

_____

5   Cathy's <u>nefew</u> will <u>giv</u> her jewelry for a <u>birthda</u> gift

_____

_____

Vocabulary Practice

Create sentences that include the vocabulary words below. Use a dictionary or electronic spell checker as needed. Underline each syllable in the vocabulary words.

9.1
claim
explain
remain
subway
entertain
maybe
complaining.
faith
spray
delay

9.2
speech
volunteer
greet
screech
pokey
freedom
donkey
week
disagree
chimney

9.3
boast
groan
float
roam
goal
rescue
argue
clue
continue
true

9.4
poison
choice
avoid
destroy
employment
fault
haunted
awkward
launch
squawk

9.5
frown
drowsy
soothing
gloomy
arrow
hook
understood
pronounce
scout
foolish

9.6
repeat
cheat
reason
dream
disappear
pleasant
steady
spread
instead
health

9.7
few
outgrew
nephew
threw
crew

Story Starter

At the end of Step 9 create a story that includes many (at least 5) of the vocabulary words below. This story is about a good dream. Underline each vocabulary word used from the list below.

dream	freedom	true	asleep
peace	continue	soar	teach
yawn	valley	afraid	cheer
drowsy	bedroom	understood	airplane
surround	window	stream	eagle

NOTES

NOTES

NOTES

NOTES

NOTES